Dog Quotes

Proverbs, Quotes & Quips

Amy Morford

This book is dedicated to dog enthusiasts everywhere.

Copyright © 2014 by Speedy Publishing LLC

All rights reserved. No part of this publication may be reproduced, distributed or transmitted in any form or by any means, including photocopying, recording, or other electronic or mechanical methods, without the prior written permission of the publisher, except in the case of brief quotations embodied in critical reviews and certain other noncommercial uses permitted by copyright law. For permission requests, write to the publisher, addressed "Attention: Permissions Coordinator," at the address below.

Speedy Publishing LLC (c) 2014
40 E. Main St., #1156
Newark, DE 19711
www.speedypublishing.co

Ordering Information:
Quantity sales; Special discounts are available on quantity purchases by corporations, associations, and others. For details, contact the "Special Sales Department" at the address above.

-- 1st edition

Manufactured in the United States of America

TABLE OF CONTENTS

PUBLISHER'S NOTES i

CHAPTER 1: A-B-C 1

CHAPTER 2: D-E-F 14

CHAPTER 3: G-H-I 20

CHAPTER 4: J-K-L 26

CHAPTER 5: M-N-O 35

CHAPTER 6: P-Q-R-S 40

CHAPTER 7: T-U-V 50

CHAPTER 8: W-X-Y-Z 53

CHAPTER 9: ANONYMOUS & UNKNOWN 57

CHAPTER 10: PROVERBS 65

CHAPTER 11: CROSS BREEDING 72

CHAPTER 12: DOG SUPERSTITIONS 73

CHAPTER 13: DOG TALES 75

MEET THE AUTHOR 81

MORE BOOKS BY AMY MORFORD 82

Publisher's Notes

Disclaimer

This publication is intended to provide helpful and informative material. It is not intended to diagnose, treat, cure, or prevent any health problem or condition, nor is intended to replace the advice of a physician. No action should be taken solely on the contents of this book. Always consult your physician or qualified health-care professional on any matters regarding your health and before adopting any suggestions in this book or drawing inferences from it.

The author and publisher specifically disclaim all responsibility for any liability, loss or risk, personal or otherwise, which is incurred as a consequence, directly or indirectly, from the use or application of any contents of this book.

Any and all product names referenced within this book are the trademarks of their respective owners. None of these owners have sponsored, authorized, endorsed, or approved this book.

Always read all information provided by the manufacturers' product labels before using their products. The author and publisher are not responsible for claims made by manufacturers.

Print Edition 2014

Chapter 1: A-B-C

<u>A</u>

When a man's best friend is his dog, that dog has a problem.
~ Edward Abbey

Dogs love company. They place it first in their short list of needs.
~ J.R. Ackerley

Well I just figure any man who risks his neck to save a dog's life isn't going to kill someone for gold teeth.
~ Alvin Adams

Barking dogs don't bite, but they themselves don't know it.
~ Sholom Aleichem

Do not disturb the sleeping dog.
~ Alessandro

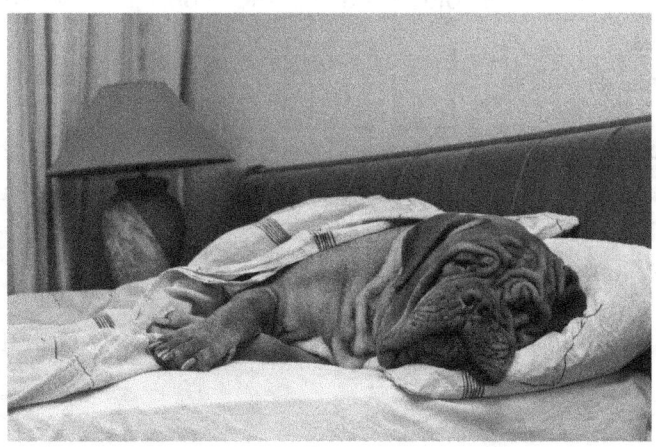

She had no particular breed in mind, no unusual requirements. Except the special sense of mutual recognition that tells dog and humans they have both come to the right place.
~ Lloyd Alexander

Old men miss many dogs.
~ Steve Allen

If you can't decide between a Shepherd, a Setter or a Poodle, get them all...adopt a mutt!
~ ASPCA

B

Truth is a good dog; but always beware of barking too close to the heels of an error, lest you get your brains kicked out.
~ Francis Bacon

Dogs travel hundreds of miles during their lifetime responding to such commands as "come" and "fetch."
~ Stephen Baker

When there is an old maid in the house, a watchdog is unnecessary.
~ Honoré de Balzac

The dog has been esteemed and loved by all the people on earth and he has deserved this affection for he renders services that have made him man's best friend.
~ Alfred Barbou

A person who has never owned a dog has missed a wonderful part of life.
~ Bob Barker

Dogs feel very strongly that they should always go with you in the car, in case the need should arise for them to bark violently at nothing right in your ear.
~ Dave Barry

Dogs love to go for rides. A dog will happily get into any vehicle going anywhere.
~ Dave Barry

Dogs need to sniff the ground; it's how they keep abreast of current events. The ground is a giant dog newspaper, containing all kinds of late-breaking dog news items, which, if they are especially urgent, are often continued in the next yard.
~ Dave Barry

The objective is not so much to walk your dog, as it is to empty him.
~ Dave Barry

You can say any fool thing to a dog, and the dog will give you this look that says, "My God, you're RIGHT! I NEVER would've thought of that!"
~ Dave Barry

DOG QUOTES

The dog is the god of frolic.
~ Henry Ward Beecher

A dog teaches a boy fidelity, perseverance, and to turn around three times before lying down.
~ Robert Benchley

The ideal age for a boy to own a dog is between forty-five and fifty.
~ Robert Benchley

The factory of the future will have only two employees, a man and a dog. The man will be there to feed the dog. The dog will be there to keep the man from touching the equipment.
~ Warren G. Bennis

I very much believe in rescuing animals, not buying them.
~ Candice Bergen

Don't let the same dog bite you twice.
~ Chuck Berry

We need another and a wiser and perhaps a more mystical concept of animals. In a world older and more complete than ours they move finished and complete, gifted with extensions of the senses we have lost or never attained, living by voices we shall never hear.

They are not brethren, they are not underlings; they are other nations, caught with ourselves in the net of life and time, fellow prisoners of the splendor and travail of the earth.
~ Harry Beston

Yet the dogs eat of the crumbs which fall from their masters' table.
~ Bible, *Matthew XV. 27*

Like a dog that returns to his vomit is a fool who repeats his folly.
~ Bible, *Proverbs XXVI. 11*

DOG, n. A subsidiary Deity designed to catch the overflow and surplus of the world's worship . . . . [H]is master works for the means wherewith to purchase the idle wag of the Solomonic tail, seasoned with a look of tolerant recognition.
~ Ambrose Bierce The Devil's Dictionary, 1911

Reverence: the spiritual attitude of a man to a god and a dog to a man.
~ Ambrose Bierce

The most affectionate creature in the world is a wet dog.
~ Ambrose Bierce

Do not wave stick when trying to catch dog.
~Earl Derr Biggers

A dog is the only thing on earth that loves you more than he loves himself.
~ Josh Billings

A puppy plays with every pup he meets, but an old dog has few associates.
~ Josh Billings

The dog that will follow everybody ain't worth a curse.
~ Josh Billings

The man who gets bit twice by the same dog is better adapted for that kind of business than any other.
~ Josh Billings

Great men have great dogs.
~ Otto von Bismarck

Hounds follow those who feed them.
~ Otto von Bismarck

Our German forefathers had a very kind religion. They believed that, after death, they would meet again all the good dogs that had been their companions in life. I wish I could believe that too.
~ Otto von Bismarck

Things that upset a terrier may pass virtually unnoticed by a Great Dane.
~ Smiley Blanton

Terrier

Did you ever notice when you blow in a dog's face he gets mad at you? But when you take him in a car he sticks his head out the window?
~ Steve Bluestein

Dogs come when they're called; cats take a message and get back to you later.
~ Mary Bly

My empty water dish mocks me.
~ Bob the Dog

When a dog bites a man that is not news, because it happens so often. But if a man bites a dog, that is news.
~ John B. Bogart

Every dog is a lion at home.
~ H.G. Bohn

When a child is locked in the bathroom with water running and he says he's doing nothing but the dog is barking, call 911.
~ Erma Bombeck

When you leave them in the morning, they stick their nose in the door crack and stand there like a portrait until you turn the key eight hours later.
~ Erma Bombeck

Youngsters of the age of two and three are endowed with extraordinary strength. They can lift a dog twice their own weight and dump him into the bathtub.
~ Erma Bombeck

There's facts about dogs, and then there's opinions about them. The dogs have the facts, and the humans have the opinions. If you want the facts about the dog, always get them straight from the dog. If you want opinions, get them from humans.
~ J. Allen Boone

Give a boy a dog and you've furnished him a playmate.
~ Berton Braley

A cat, after being scolded, goes about its business. A dog slinks off into a corner and pretends to be doing a serious self-reappraisal.
~ Robert Brault

An old dog, even more than an old spouse, always feels like doing what you feel like doing.
~ Robert Brault

Ever wonder where you'd end up if you took your dog for a walk and never once pulled back on the leash?
~ Robert Brault

I am not your dog, but if every time you saw me, you gave me a backrub, I would run to greet you, too.
~ Robert Brault

The Airedale... an unrivaled mixture of brains and clownish wit, the very ingredients one looks for in a spouse.
~ Chip Brown

Airedale Terrier

If there is a heaven, it's certain our animals are to be there. Their lives become so interwoven with our own; it would take more than an archangel to detangle them.
~ Pam Brown

A dog is not considered a good dog because he is a good barker. A man is not considered a good man because he is a good talker.
~ Buddha

I'd rather have an inch of a dog than a mile of pedigree.
~ Dana Burnet

The great pleasure of a dog is that you may make a fool of yourself with him and not only will he not scold you, but he will make a fool of himself too.
~ Samuel Butler

A dog wags its tail with its heart.
~ Martin Buxbaum

C

You learn in this business: It you want a friend, get a dog.
~ Carl I Cahn, US Auto Business Executive

Only my dogs will not betray me.
~ Maria Callas

If dogs could talk, perhaps we would find it as hard to get along with them as we do with people.
~ Capek

Dogs are not our whole life, but they make our lives whole.
~ Roger Caras

DOG QUOTES

Dogs have given us their absolute all. We are the center of their universe. We are the focus of their love and faith and trust. They serve us in return for scraps. It is without a doubt the best deal man has ever made.
~ Roger Caras

For me a house or an apartment becomes a home when you add one set of four legs, a happy tail, and that indescribable measure of love that we call a dog.
~ Roger Caras

I am confounded by dogs as I am indebted to them.
~ Roger Caras

If you don't own a dog, at least one, there is not necessarily anything wrong with you, but there may be something wrong with your life.
~ Roger Caras

Some of our greatest historical and artistic treasures we place with curators in museums; others we take for walks.
~ Roger Caras

We derive immeasurable good, uncounted pleasures, enormous security, and many critical lessons about life by owning dogs.
~ Roger Caras

"Meow" means "woof" in cat.
~ George Carlin

What do dogs do on their day off? Can't lie around – that's their job!
~ George Carlin

The cat is the mirror of his human's mind...the dog mirrors his human's physical appearance.
~ Winnifred Carriere

Men cheat for the same reason that dogs lick their balls...because they can.
~ Kim Cattrall, as Samantha Jones in *Sex and the City*

I have a great dog. She's half Lab, half pit bull. A good combination. Sure, she might bite off my leg, but she'll bring it back to me.
~ Jimi Celeste

The Life of an uneducated man is as useless as the tail of a dog which neither covers its rear end, nor protects it from the bites of insects.
~ Chanakya

Flatters look like friends, as wolves like dogs.
~ George Chapman

Love me, love my dog.
~ George Chapman

The dog represents all that is best in man.
~ Etienne Charlet

DOG QUOTES

I always like a dog so long as he isn't spelled backward.
~ G.K. Chesterton

Dogs are wise. They crawl away into a quiet corner and lick their wounds and do not rejoin the world until they are whole once more.
~ Agatha Christie

The nose of the bulldog has been slanted backwards so that he can breathe without letting go.
~ Winston Churchill

Dogs wait for us faithfully.
~ Marcus Tullius Cicero

I know that dogs are pack animals, but it's difficult to imagine a pack of standard poodles . . . and if there was such a thing as a pack of standard poodles, where would they rove to? Bloomingdale's?
~ Yvonne Clifford

Sometimes I feel like a fire hydrant looking at a pack of dogs.
~ Bill Clinton

Nobody else feels the same way about your dog that you do.
~ Daniel Clowes

I could discern clearly, even at that early age, the essential difference between people who are *kind* to dogs and people who really *love* them.
~ Frances P. Cobbe

Everyone's pet is the most outstanding. This begets mutual blindness.
~ Jean Cocteau

Every year the State will be the dog that chases its own tail...engaging in a futile attempt to close a perpetual budget gap.
~ Richard J. Codey

I confronted the fact that I was not only talking to a dog, but answering for one.
~ Claire Cook

I never married because...I have three pets at home which answer the same purpose as a husband. I have a dog which growls every morning, a parrot which swears all afternoon, and a cat that come home late at night.
~ Marie Corelli

The dog has no ambition, no self-interest, no desire for vengeance, no fear other than that of displeasing.
~ Count of Buffon

If you get to thinkin' you're a person of some influence, try orderin' somebody else's dog around.
~ Cowboy Wisdom

My cats inspire me daily. They inspire me to get a dog.
~ Greg Curtis

Chapter 2: D-E-F

_D_

There's a saying. If you want someone to love you forever, buy a dog, feed it and keep it around.
~ Dick Dale

I looked up my family tree and found three dogs using it.
~ Rodney Dangerfield

It's tough to stay married. My wife kisses the dog on the lips, yet she won't drink from my glass.
~ Rodney Dangerfield

What a dog I got, his favorite bone is in my arm.
~ Rodney Dangerfield

It is scarcely possible to doubt that the love of man has become instinctive in the dog.
~ Charles Darwin

Man himself cannot express love and humility by external signs, so plainly as does a dog, when with drooping ears, hanging lips, flexuous body, and wagging tail, he meets his beloved master.
~ Charles Darwin

A good dog never dies. He always stays. He walks besides you on crisp autumn days when frost is on the fields and winter's drawing near. His head is within our hand in his old way.
~ Mary Carolyn Davies

I have found that when you are deeply troubled, there are things you get from the silent devoted companionship of a dog that you can get from no other source.
~ Doris Day

The only creatures that are evolved enough to convey pure love are dogs and infants.
~ Johnny Depp

A dog is the only thing that can mend a crack in your broken heart.
~ Judy Desmond

It's hard not to immediately fall in love with a dog who has a good sense of humor.
~ Kate DiCamillo

You can always trust a dog that likes peanut butter.
~ Kate DiCamillo

Let sleeping dogs lie.
~ Charles Dickens

This alpha dog is not going to take it lying down next time.
~ Janice Dickinson

DOG QUOTES

Every time I go near the stove, the dog howls...
~ Phyllis Diller

Our dog died from licking our wedding picture.
~ Phyllis Diller

Dogs and philosophers do the greatest good and get the fewest rewards.
~ Diogenes

I am called a dog because I fawn on those who give me anything, I yelp at those who refuse, and I set my teeth in rascals.
~ Diogenes

What's the difference between a 3-week-old puppy and a sportswriter? In 6 weeks, the puppy will stop whining.
~ Mike Ditka

My dear old dog, most constant of all friends.
~ William Croswell Doane

Dogs are, after all, man's best friend. The least we can do is try to understand them a little better.
~ Nicholas Dodman

All of the good things that have come to me have come through my dog.
~ Dog owner overheard in New York's Central Park

A man's soul can be judged by the way he treats his dog.
~ Charles Doran

Rambunctious, rumbustious, delinquent dogs become angelic when sitting.
~ Dr. Ian Dunbar

The best way to make friends with a dog is to talk to him. He can't talk back, but he can understand a heap more than you think he can.
~ Walter A. Dyer

E

Dogs laugh, but they laugh with their tails.
~ Max Eastman

You enter into a certain amount of madness when you marry a person with pets.
~ Nora Ephron

When dogs leap onto your bed, it's because they adore being with you. When cats leap onto your bed, it's because they adore your bed.
~ Alisha Everett

The average dog has one request to all humankind. Love me.
~ Helen Exley

F

If you want loyalty, get a dog. If you want loyalty and attention, get a smart dog.
~ Grant Fairley

The dog is mentioned in the Bible eighteen times - the cat not even once.
~ W.E. Farbstein

In dog training, jerk is a noun, not a verb.
~ Dr. Dennis Fetko

If your dog thinks you're the greatest person in the world, don't seek a second opinion.
~ Jim Fiebig

DOG QUOTES

You own a dog; you feed a cat.
~ Jim Fiebig

Every dog should have a man of his own. There is nothing like a well-behaved person around the house to spread the dog's blanket for him, or bring him his supper when he comes home man-tired at night.
~ Corey Ford

Properly trained, a man can be a dog's best friend.
~ Corey Ford

Dogs teach us a very important lesson in life: The mail man is not to be trusted.
~Sian Ford

Watching a baby being born is a little like watching a wet St. Bernard coming in through the cat door.
~ Jeff Foxworthy

St. Bernard

There are three faithful friends - an old wife, an old dog, and ready money.
~ Benjamin Franklin

Dogs love their friends and bite their enemies, quite unlike people, who are incapable of pure love and always have to mix love and hate.
~ Sigmund Freud

The scientific name for an animal that doesn't either run from or fight its enemies is lunch.
~ Michael Friedman

Chapter 3: G-H-I

_G_

Not the least hard thing to bear when they go from us, these quiet friends, is that they carry away with them so many years of our own lives.
~ John Galsworthy

I guess you don't really own a dog, you rent them, and you have to be thankful that you had a long lease.
~ Joe Garagiola

You really have to be some kind of a creep for a dog to reject you.
~ Joe Garagiola

If you have a dog, you will most likely outlive it; to get a dog is to open yourself to profound joy and, prospectively, to equally profound sadness.
~ Marjorie Garber

Who can believe that there is no soul behind the luminous eyes of a dog.
~ Theophile Gautier

Amount of time it takes for a dog to "do its business" is directly proportional to outside temperature + suitability of owner's outerwear.
~ Betsy Cañas Garmon

The gift which I am sending you is called a dog, and is in fact the most precious and valuable possession of mankind.
~ Theodorus Gaza

A leaky faucet, a barking dog – those are things you tolerate.
~ Candace Gingrich

Do you know there is always a barrier between me and any man or woman who does not like dogs?
~ Ellen Glasgow

And then there's the personal question so many of Lassie's fans want to ask: Is he allowed on the furniture? Of course he is – but, then, he's the one who paid for it.
~ Julia Glass

When most of us talk to our dogs, we tend to forget they're not people.
~ Julia Glass

I don't think twice about picking up my dog's poop, but if another dog's poop is next to it, I think, "Eww, dog poop!"
~ Jonah Goldberg

He has every attribute of a dog except loyalty.
~ Senator Thomas P. Gore

Old age means realizing you will never own all the dogs you wanted to.
~ Joe Gores

God will prepare everything for our perfect happiness in heaven, and if it takes my dog being there, I believe he'll be there.
~ Rev. Billy Graham

The one absolutely unselfish friend that man can have in this selfish world, the one that never deserts him, the one that never proves ungrateful or treacherous, is his dog.
~ George Graham

DOG QUOTES

A dog desires affection more than its dinner. Well – almost.
~ Charlotte Gray

Life is like a dog sled team. If you ain't the lead dog, the scenery never changes.
~ Lewis Grizzard

View If You Ain't the Lead Dog

A dog with seven toes can see ghosts.
~ Matt Groening

A dog is the greatest gift a parent can give a child. OK, a good education, then a dog.
~ John Grogan

Not only is life a bitch, but it is always having puppies.
~ Adrienne Gusoff

<u>H</u>

Asking a working writer what he thinks about critics is like asking a lamp-post how it feels about dogs.
~ Christopher Hampton

I like any dog that makes me look good when it stands next to me.
~ Jean Harlow

The great tie that binds us to dogs is not their fidelity or their charm or anything else but the fact that they are not critical of us.
~ Sydney J. Harris

They motivate us to play, be affectionate, seek adventure and be loyal.
~ Tom Hayden

People teach their dogs to sit; it's a trick. I've been sitting my whole life, and a dog has never looked at me as though he thought I was tricky.
~ Mitch Hedberg

It's a dog eat dog world, and Mr. Perfect is a Milk Bone.
~ Bobby Heenan

Dogs act exactly the way we would act if we had no shame.
~ Cynthia Heimel

Women and cats will do as they please and men and dogs should relax and get used to the idea.
~ Robert A. Heinlein

In modern war...you will die like a dog for no good reason.
~ Ernest Hemingway

I'm half-Irish, half-Dutch, and I was born in Belgium. If I was a dog, I'd be in a hell of a mess!
~ Audrey Hepburn

Even the smallest dog can lift its leg on the tallest building.
~ Jim Hightower

DOG QUOTES

I can't think of anything that brings me closer to tears than when my old dog - completely exhausted after a hard day in the field - limps away from her nice spot in front of the fire and comes over to where I'm sitting and puts her head in my lap, a paw over my knee, and closes her eyes and goes back to sleep. I don't know what I've done to deserve that kind of friend.
~ Gene Hill

We never really own a dog as much as he owns us.
~ Gene Hill

Whoever said you can't buy happiness forgot about little puppies.
~ Gene Hill

Even the tiniest poodle or Chihuahua is still a wolf at heart.
~ Dorthy Patent Hinshaw

Chihuahua

In order to really enjoy a dog, one doesn't merely try to train him to be semi human. The point of it is to open oneself to the possibility of becoming partly a dog.
~ Edward Hoagland

Lots of people talk to animals...Not very many listen, though...That's the problem.
~ Benjamin Hoff

A dog is not "almost human," and I know of no greater insult to the canine race than to describe it as such.
~ John Holmes

You may have a dog that won't sit up, roll over or even cook breakfast, not because she's too stupid to learn how but because she's too smart to bother.
~ Rick Horowitz

To his dog, every man is Napoleon; hence the constant popularity of dogs.
~ Aldous Huxley

!

There are times when even the best manager is like the little boy with the big dog. Waiting to see where the dog wants to go so he can take him there.
~ Lee Iacocca

My dog is usually pleased with what I do, because she is not infected with the concept of what I "should" be doing.
~ Lonzo Idolswine

Chapter 4: J-K-L

_J_

Man is a dog's idea of what God should be.
~ Holbrook Jackson

Fox-terriers are born with about four times as much original sin in them as other dogs.
~Jerome K. Jerome

He never makes it his business to inquire whether you are in the right or wrong, never bothers as to whether you are going up or down life's ladder, never asks whether you are rich or poor, silly or wise, sinner or saint. You are his pal. That is enough for him.
~ Jerome K. Jerome

They [dogs] never talk about themselves but listen to you while you talk about yourself, and keep up an appearance of being interested in the conversation.
~ Jerome K. Jerome

Dogs have not the power of comparing. A dog will take a small piece of meat as readily as a large, when both are before him.
~ Samuel Johnson

I would rather see the portrait of a dog that I know, than all the allegorical paintings they can show me in the world.
~ Samuel Johnson

Anybody who doesn't know what soap tastes like never washed a dog.
~ Franklin P. Jones

Scratch a dog and you'll find a permanent job.
~ Franklin P. Jones

If you're being chased by a police dog, try not to go through a tunnel, then on to a little seesaw, then jump through a hoop of fire. They're trained for that.
~ Milton Jones

Dogs have a way of finding the people who need them, filling an emptiness we don't even know we have.
~ Thom Jones

Who kicks a dog kicks his own soul towards hell.
~ Will Judy

I used to look at Smokey and think, "If you were a little smarter you could tell me what you were thinking," and he'd look at me like he was saying, "If you were a little smarter, I wouldn't have to."
~ Fred Jungclaus

_K_

All knowledge, the totality of all questions and answers, is contained in the dog.
~ Franz Kafk

DOG QUOTES

A dog is like an eternal Peter Pan, a child who never grows old and who therefore is always available to love and be loved.
~ Aaron Katcher

For a man living alone dogs are almost more important than human beings.
~ Richard Katz

The pug is living proof that God has a sense of humor.
~ Margo Kaufman

Pug

One of the most enduring friendships in history – dogs and their people, people and their dogs.
~ Terry Kay

Dogs are miracles with paws.
~ Attributed to Susan Ariel Rainbow Kennedy

Buy a pup and your money will buy love unflinching.
~ Rudyard Kipling

His name is not wild dog anymore, but the first friend, because he will be our friend for always and always and always.
~ Rudyard Kipling

The dog's agenda is simple, fathomable, overt: I want. "I want to go out, come in, eat something, lie here, play with that, kiss you." There are no ulterior motives with a dog, no mind games, no second-guessing, no complicated negotiations or bargains, and no guilt trips or grudges if a request is denied.
~ Caroline Knapp

Intelligent dogs rarely want to please people whom they do not respect.
~ W.R. Koehler

Petting, scratching, and cuddling a dog could be as soothing to the mind and heart as deep meditation and almost as good for the soul as prayer.
~ Dean Koontz

Everyone needs a spiritual guide: a minister, rabbi, counselor, wise friend, or therapist. My own wise friend is my dog.
~ Gary Kowalski

My dog does have his failing, of course. He's afraid of firecrackers and hides in the clothes closet whenever we run the vacuum cleaner, but, unlike me he's not afraid of what other people think of him or anxious about his public image.
~ Gary Kowalski

Jealousy is a dog's bark which attracts thieves.
~ Karl Kraus

Sentimental irony is a dog that bays at the moon while pissing on graves.
~ Karl Kraus

Dogs are our link to paradise. They don't know evil or jealousy or discontent. To sit with a dog on a hillside on a glorious afternoon is to be back in Eden, where doing nothing was not boring - it was peace.
~ Milan Kundera

The dog is like a liberal. He wants to please everybody.
~ William Kunstler

L

The more I see of the depressing stature of people, the more I admire my dogs.
~ Alphonse de Lamartine

The one best place to bury a good dog is in the heart of his master.
~ Ben Hur Lampman

Owning a dog is slightly less expensive than being addicted to crack.
~ Jen Lancaster

Know yourself. Don't accept your dog's admiration as conclusive evidence that you are wonderful.
~ Ann Landers

If a pit bull romances your leg, fake an orgasm.
~ Hut Landon

Pit Bull

But in order to be the thing you want to be, you have to work like a dog at the thing you love.
~ Frank Langella

Home computers are being called upon to perform many new functions, including the consumption of homework formerly eaten by the dog.
~ Doug Larson

Nothing but love has made the dog lose his wild freedom, to become the servant of man.
~ D.H. Lawrence

DOG QUOTES

If you are a dog and your owner suggests that you wear a sweater. . . suggest that he wear a tail.
~ Fran Lebowitz

No animal should ever jump up on the dining-room furniture unless absolutely certain that he can hold his own in the conversation.
~ Fran Lebowitz

I've been on so many blind dates, I should get a free dog.
~ Wendy Liebman

My mom was a ventriloquist and she always was throwing her voice. For ten years I thought the dog was telling me to kill my father.
~ Wendy Liebman

No animal I know of can consistently be more of a friend and companion than a dog.
~ Stanley Leinwoll

How many legs does a dog have if you call the tail a leg? Four. Calling a tail a leg doesn't make it a leg.
~ Abraham Lincoln

I care not for a man's religion whose dog and cat are not the better for it.
~ Abraham Lincoln

Killing the dog does not cure the bite.
~ Abraham Lincoln

A bone to the dog is not charity. Charity is the bone shared with the dog, when you are just as hungry as the dog.
~ Jack London

It all started when my dog began getting free roll over minutes.
~ Jay London

The poor dog, in life the firmest friend. The first to welcome, foremost to defend.
~ Lord Bryon

The fidelity of a dog is a precious gift demanding no less binding moral responsibilities than the friendship of a human being. The bond with a dog is as lasting as the ties of this earth can ever be.
~ Konrad Lorenz

The plain fact that my dog loves me more than I love her is undeniable, and always fills me with a certain amount of shame.
~ Konrad Lorenz

There is no faith which has never yet been broken, except that of a truly faithful dog.
~ Konrad Lorenz

People leave imprints on our lives, shaping who we become in much the same way that a symbol is pressed into the page of a book to tell you who it comes from. Dogs, however, leave paw prints on our lives and our souls, which are as unique as fingerprints in every way.
~ Ashly Lorenzana

DOG QUOTES

The difference between dogs and men is that you know where dogs sleep at night.
~ Greg Louganis

You think dogs will not be in heaven? I tell you, they will be there long before any of us.
~ Robert Louis

Muzzle a dog and he will bark out of the other end.
~ Malcolm Lowry

Chapter 5: M-N-O

<u>M</u>

The dog who meets with a good master is the happier of the two.
~ Maurice Maeterlinck

We are alone, absolutely alone on his chance planet, and amid all the forms of life that surround us, not one, excepting the dog, have made an alliance with us.
~ Maurice Maeterlinck

Thorns may hurt you, men desert you, sunlight turn to fog; But you're never friendless ever, if you have a dog.
~ Douglas Mallock

I sometimes look into the face of my dog Stan and see a wistful sadness and existential angst, when all he is actually doing is slowly scanning the ceiling for flies.
~ Merrill Markoe

If your house burns down, rescue the dogs. At least they'll be faithful to you.
~ Lee Marvin

Just give me a comfortable couch, a dog, a good book, and a woman. Then if you can get the dog to go somewhere and read the book, I might have a little fun!
~ Groucho Marx

Outside of a dog, a book is probably man's best friend, and inside of a dog, it's too dark to read.
~ Groucho Marx

DOG QUOTES

Dogs never lie about love.
~ Jeffrey Moussaieff Masson

Perhaps one central reason for loving dogs is that they take us away from this obsession with ourselves. When our thoughts start to go in circles, and we seem unable to break away, wondering what horrible event the future holds for us, the dog opens a window into the delight of the moment.
~ Jeffrey Moussaieff Masson

We might miss the sign or we may be unable to read the expression, but it is almost a contradiction in terms to say that a dog feels something but does not show it. What a dog feels, a dog shows, and, conversely, what a dog shows, a dog actually does feel.
~ Jeffrey Moussaieff Masson

It has been 20,000 years since man and dog formed their partnership.
~ Donald McCaig

Show me a dog who still cannot perform a task after it has been trained over and over again, and I'll tell you who the slow learner is.
~ Barry McDonald

Isn't it wonderful how dogs can win friends and influence people without ever reading a book.
~ E.C. McKenzie

The dog that trots about finds a bone.
~ Golda Meir

A professor must have a theory as a dog must have fleas.
~H.L. Mencken

Dachshund: A half-a-dog high and a dog-and-a-half long.
~H.L. Mencken

Living with a dog is easy – like living with an idealist.
~H.L. Mencken

Of all the animals, surely the dog is the only one that really shares our life, helps in our work, and has a place in our recreation. It is the only one that becomes so fond of us that sometimes it cannot go on living after its master dies.
~ Fernand Mercy

I believe in integrity. Dogs have it. Humans are sometimes lacking it.
~ Cesar Millan

The biggest dog has been a pup.
~ Joaquin Miller

Aristocrats have heirs, the poor have children, and the rest keep dogs.
~ Spike Milligan

Speak softly and own a big, mean Doberman.
~Dave Millman

Doberman

DOG QUOTES

A lover tires to stand in well with the pet dog of the house.
~ Moliere

Have you hugged your pug today?
~ Marty Moose

No one appreciates the very special genius of your conversation as the dog does.
~ Christopher Morley

I wonder what goes through his mind when he sees us peeing in his water bowl.
~ Penny Ward Moser

Did you ever walk into a room and forget why you walked in? I think that is how dogs spend their lives.
~ Sue Murphy

N

A door is what a dog is perpetually on the wrong side of.
~ Ogden Nash

Love is the emotion that a woman feels always for a poodle dog and sometimes for a man.
~ George Jean Nathan

A dog is for life, and not just for Christmas.
~ National Canine Defense League slogan

Who knew that dog saliva can mend a broken heart?
~ Jennifer Neal

It's a dog eat dog world, and I'm wearing Milk Bone underwear.
~ Norm, from Cheer's

O

Any woman who does not thoroughly enjoy tramping across the country on a clear frosty morning with a good gun and a pair of dogs does not know how to enjoy life.
~ Annie Oakley

Revenge is often like biting a dog because the dog bit you.
~ Austin O'Malley

Dogs...do not ruin their sleep worrying about how to keep the objects they have, and to obtain the objects they have not. There is nothing of value they have to bequeath except their love and their faith.
~ Eugene O'Neill

Great men always have dogs.
~ Ouida

Chapter 6: P-Q-R-S

<u>P</u>

Leaving sex to the feminists is like letting your dog vacation at the taxidermist.
~ Camille Paglia

When you feel lousy, puppy therapy is indicated.
~ Sara Paretsky

The conclusion I have reached is that, above all, dogs are witnesses. They are allowed access to our most private moments. They are there when we think we are alone. Think of what they could tell us. They sit on the laps of presidents. They see acts of love and violence, quarrels and feuds, and the secret play of children. If they could tell us everything they have seen, all of the gaps of our lives would stitch themselves together.
~ Carolyn Parkhurst

I look at myself like a show dog. I've got to keep her clipped and trimmed and in good shape.
~ Dolly Parton

If you think dogs can't count, try putting three dog biscuits in your pocket and then giving Fido only two of them.
~Phil Pastoret

Dogs give their human companions unconditional love and are always there with an encouraging wag of the tail when they are needed. The dog is indeed a very special animal.
~ Dorthy Hinshaw Patent

Dog is the only animal in the world who ostensibly like another breed better than his own. Man.
~ Ted Patrick

You kick a dog long enough, that dog is going to bite you or die.
~ Dave Pelzer

The best way to get a puppy is to beg for a baby brother - and they'll settle for a puppy every time.
~ Winston Pendelton

I have days when I just feel I look like a dog.
~ Michelle Pfeiffer

Happiness is dog-shaped, I say.
~ Chapman Pincher

The old saw about old dogs and new tricks only applies to certain people.
~ Daniel Pinkwater

A dog has the soul of a philosopher.
~ Plato

DOG QUOTES

Histories are more full of examples of the fidelity of dogs than of friends.
~ Alexander Pope

No louder shrieks to pitying heaven are cast,
When husbands or lap-dogs breathe their last.
~ Alexander Pope

Sooner or later we're all someone's dog.
~ Terry Pratchett

_Q_

_R_

Keep running after a dog and he will never bite you.
~ Francois Rabelais

I think dogs are the most amazing creatures; they give unconditional love. For me they are the role model for being alive.
~ Gilda Radner

The best way to get over a dog's death is to get another soon.
~ Ronald Reagan

They say the dog is man's best friend. I don't believe that. How many of your friends have you neutered?
~ Larry Reeb

Gratitude: that quality which the Canine Mongrel seldom lacks; which the Human Mongrel seldom possesses!
~ Lion P.S. Rees

A puppy is but a dog, plus high spirits, and minus common sense.
~ Agnes Repplier

Our dogs will love and admire the meanest of us, and feed our colossal vanity with their uncritical homage.
~ Agnes Repplier

One of the happiest sights in the world comes when a lost dog is reunited with a master he loves. You just haven't seen joy till you have seen that.
~ Eldon Roark

Everything I know, I learned from dogs.
~ Nora Roberts

From the dog's point of view, his master is an elongated and abnormally cunning dog.
~ Mabel Louise Robinson

My Scottie refused to go for a walk with a friend of the house, but she would joyously accompany any stranger who drove a car.
~ Mazo de la Roche

I love a dog. He does nothing for political reasons.
~ Will Rogers

DOG QUOTES

No man can be condemned for owning a dog. As long as he has a dog, he has a friend; and the poorer he gets, the better friend he has.
~ Will Rogers

The time to save is now. When a dog gets a bone, he doesn't go out and make a down payment on a bigger bone. He buries the one he's got.
~ Will Rogers

If dogs could talk it would take a lot of the fun out of owning one.
~ Andy Rooney

The average dog is a nicer person than the average person.
~ Andy. Rooney

I'm no one's lap dog; you can't put me on a leash.
~ Johnny Rotten

Breaks balance out. The sun don't shine on the same ol' dog's rear end every day.
~ Darrell Royal

I wonder if other dogs think poodles are members of a weird religious cult.
~ Rita Rudner

Poodle

My husband and I are either going to buy a dog or have a child. We can't decide whether to ruin our carpets or ruin our lives.
~ Rita Rudner

We've begun to long for the pitter-patter of little feet - so we bought a dog. Well, it's cheaper, and you get more feet.
~ Rita Rudner

S

Even the tiniest poodle is lionhearted, ready to do anything to defend home, master, and mistress.
~ Louis Sabin

No matter how little money and how few possessions you own, having a dog makes you rich.
~ Louis Sabin

I once decided not to date a guy because he wasn't excited to meet my dog. I mean, this was like not wanting to meet my mother.
~ Bonnie Schacter

The little furry buggers are just deep, deep wells you throw all your emotions into.
~ Bruce Schimmel

Bite us once, shame on the dog; bite us repeatedly, shame on us for allowing it.
~ Phyllis Schlafly

There's just something about dogs that makes you feel good. You come home, they're thrilled to see you. They're good for the ego.
~ Janet Schnellman

All his life he tried to be a good person. Many times, however, he failed. For after all, he was only human. He wasn't a dog.
~ Charles M. Schulz

DOG QUOTES

Happiness is a warm puppy.
~ Charles M. Schulz

That's the only dog I know who can smell someone just *thinking* about food.
~ Charles M. Schulz

Do not make the mistake of treating your dogs like humans or they will treat you like dogs.
~ Martha Scott

Hunger and fear are the only realities in dog life: an empty stomach makes a fierce dog.
~ Robert F. Scott

The dog lives for the day, the hour, even the moment.
~ Robert F. Scott

With great care we might have a dog's chance, but no more.
~ Robert F. Scott

The misery of keeping a dog is his dying so soon. But, to be sure, if he lived for fifty years and then died, what would become of me?
~ Sir Walter Scott

It is much easier to show compassion to animals. They are never wicked.
~ Haile Selassie

It is true that whenever a person loves a dog he derives great power from it.
~ Old Seneca Chief

Not Carnegie, Vanderbilt and Astor together could have raised money enough to buy a quarter share in my little dog.
~ Ernest Thompson Seton

Blessed is the person who has earned the love of an old dog.
~ Sidney Jeanne Seward

Nature teaches beasts to know their friends.
~ William Shakespeare

The dog doesn't know the difference between Saturday, Sunday, and Monday, so I have to walk the dog early those days too.
~ Donna Shalala

If I loved a guy as much as I love my dog, the guy would be in serious trouble. Because I'm all over that dog, all the time.
~ Maria Sharapova

Money will buy you a pretty good dog, but it won't buy the wag of his tail.
~ Henry Wheeler Shaw

None are as fiercely loyal as dog people. In return, no doubt, for the never-ending loyalty of dogs.
~ Linda Shrieves, Orlando Sentinel

Acquiring a dog may be the only opportunity a human ever has to choose a relative.
~ Mordecai Siegal

A dog is not intelligent. Never trust an animal that is surprised by its own farts.
~ Frank Skinner

Man is an animal that makes bargains: no other animal does this – no dog exchanges bones with another.
~ Adam Smith

Yesterday I was a dog. Today I'm a dog. Tomorrow I'll probably still be a dog. Sigh! There's so little hope for advancement.
~ Snoopy

DOG QUOTES

Parrots, tortoises and redwoods live a longer life than men do; Men a longer life than dogs do; dogs a longer life than love does.
~ Edna St. Vincent Millay

The more I see of man, the more I like dogs.
~ Mme. de Staël

Getting a dog is like getting married. It teaches you to be less self-centered, to accept sudden, surprising outbursts of affection, and not to be upset by a few scratches on your car.
~ Will Stanton

A dog is a bond between strangers.
~ John Steinbeck

I've seen a look in dogs' eyes, a quickly vanishing look of amazed contempt, and I am convinced that basically dogs think humans are nuts.
~ John Steinbeck

On the internet, nobody knows you're a dog.
~ Peter Steiner

There are more dog owners in America than there are conservatives.
~ Roger Stone

If I had the choice of having the company of a person or a dog, I would just as soon be with the dog.
~ Chuck Straub

I loathe people who keep dogs. They are cowards who haven't got the guts to bite people themselves.
~ August Strindberg

Labradors [are] lousy watchdogs. They usually bark when there is a stranger about, but it is an expression of unmitigated joy at the chance to meet somebody new, not a warning.
~Norman Strung

Most dogs don't think that they are human; they know they are.
~ Jane Swan

Every dog must have his day.
~ Jonathan Swift

Chapter 7: T-U-V

T

Dog lovers are a good breed themselves.
~ Gladys Taber

Some of my best leading men have been dogs and horses.
~ Elizabeth Taylor

When a puppy takes fifty catnaps in the course of the day, he cannot always be expected to sleep the night through.
~ Albert Payson Terhune

A well-trained dog will make no attempt to share your lunch. He will just make you feel so guilty that you cannot enjoy it.
~ Helen Thomson

Inside every Newfoundland, Boxer, Elkhound and Great Dane is a puppy longing to climb on to your lap.
~ Helen Thomson

When a dog runs at you, whistle for him.
~ Henry David Thoreau

I have always thought of a dog lover as a dog that was in love with another dog.
~ James Thurber

If I have any beliefs about immortality, it is that certain dogs I have known will go to heaven, and very, very few persons.
~ James Thurber

The more one gets to know of men, the more one values dogs.
~ Alphonse Toussenel

Children and dogs are as necessary to the welfare of the country as Wall Street and the railroads.
~ Harry S Truman

You want a friend in Washington? Get a dog.
~ Harry S. Truman

Dogs' lives are too short. Their only fault, really.
~ Agnes Sligh Turnbull

Heaven goes by favor. If it went by merit, you would stay out and your dog would go in.
~ Mark Twain

If animals could speak, the dog would be a blundering outspoken fellow; but the cat would have the rare grace of never saying a word too much.
~ Mark Twain

If you pick up a starving dog and make him prosperous, he will not bite you; that is the principal difference between a dog and a man.
~ Mark Twain

It's not the size of the dog in the fight, it's the size of the fight in the dog.
~ Mark Twain

The dog is a gentleman; I hope to go to his heaven, not man's.
~ Mark Twain

DOG QUOTES

Ever consider what they must think of us? I mean, here we come back from a grocery store with the most amazing haul- chicken, pork, half cow. They must think we're the greatest hunters on earth!
~ Anne Tyler

U

A piece of grass a day keeps the vet away.
~ Unknown Dog

V

A dog is like a person—he needs a job and a family to be what he's meant to be.
~ Andrew Vachss

My dogs forgive anger in me, the arrogance in me, the brute in me. They forgive everything I do before I forgive myself.
~ Guy de la Valdene

Cats are smarter than dogs. You can't get eight cats to pull a sled through snow.
~ Jeff Valdez

Stick around any place long enough and chances are you'll be taken for granted. Hang around 20,000 years wagging your tail and being man's (and woman's) best friend, and you'll be taken for granted big time.
~ Lynn Van Matre

You can tell by the kindness of a dog how a human should be.
~ Don Van Vliet

Chapter 8: W-X-Y-Z

_W_

A dog will teach you unconditional love. If you can have that in your life, things won't be too bad.
~ Robert Wagner

I know that I have had friends who would never have vexed or betrayed me, if they had walked on all fours.
~ Horace Walpole

I'm like an old dog, I hate to be run off from home.
~ Doc Watson

It takes a strong minded human to appreciate a string-minded dog!
~ Mary Webber

Cowardly dogs bark loudest.
~ John Webster

If my dog is barred by the heavenly guard
We'll both of us brave the heat!
~ W. Dayton Wedgefarth

My dog is worried about the economy because Alpo is up to 99 cents a can. That's almost $7.00 in dog money.
~ Joe Weinstein

My little dog - a heartbeat at my feet.
~ Edith Wharton

DOG QUOTES

A really companionable and indispensable dog is an accident of nature. You can't get it by breeding for it, and you can't buy it with money. It just happens.
~ E.B. White

Old dogs, like old shoes, are comfortable. They might be a bit out of shape and a little worn around the edges, but they fit well.
~ Bonnie Wilcox

The dog without his master was like a body without a soul.
~ Mary E. Wilkins

There is no psychiatrist in the world like a puppy licking your face.
~ Ben Williams

No symphony orchestra ever played music like a two-year-old girl laughing with a puppy.
~ Bern Williams

The dog and the rabbit are telling us not to chase unattainable material goals.
~ Kit Williams

It is a terrible thing for an old woman to outlive her dogs.
~ Tennessee Williams

They give unconditional love and undying loyalty in return for regular meals and an occasional pat on the head.
~ Jon Winokur

To a dog, motoring isn't just a way of getting from here to there, it's also a thrill and an adventure. The mere jingle of car keys is enough to send most any dog into a whimpering, tail-wagging frenzy.
~ Jon Winokur

It is fatal to let any dog know that he is funny, for he immediately losses his head and starts hamming it up.
~ P.G. Wodehouse

Why do dachshunds wear their ears inside out?
~ P.G. Wodehouse

Many dogs will give a greeting grin much like a human smile.
~ Richard A. Wolters

I can train any dog in 5 minutes. It's training the owner that takes longer.
~ Barbara Woodhouse

I have caught more ills from people sneezing over me and giving me virus infections than from kissing dogs.
~ Barbara Woodhouse

I poured spot remover on my dog. Now he's gone.
~ Steven Wright

DOG QUOTES

X & Y

Z

Never have I experienced a serenity and a sweetness of disposition as with my Chocolate Lab.
~ Mortimer B. Zuckerman

Chocolate Labrador Retriever Puppy

Chapter 9: Anonymous & Unknown

A boy's best friend is his dog.

A cat sees us as the dogs and himself as the human.

A dog's bark may be worse than his bite, but it's never quite so personal.

A dog can express more with his tail in minutes than his owner can express with his tongue in hours.

A dog doesn't care if you're rich or poor, educated or illiterate, clever or dull. Give him your heart and he will give you his.

A dog is man's best friend, and vice versa.

A dog is one of the remaining reasons why some people can be persuaded to go for a walk.

A dog will quickly turn you into a fool, but who cares? Better your dog than your boss.

A house is not a home without a dog.

A hungry dog hunts best.

A spoiled rotten dog lives here.

A watchdog is a dog kept to guard your home, usually by sleeping where a burglar would awaken the household by falling over him.

Actually, your watch dog guards his own home and incidentally yours.

Barking dogs seldom bite.

DOG QUOTES

Barking up the wrong tree.

Be tuff! The "dog days" of summer can be wuff!

Being patted is what it is all about.

Cat's Motto: No matter what you've done wrong, always try to make it look like the dog did it.

Chasing your tail gets you nowhere...'cept back to where you started.

Cleaning with dogs in your house is like brushing your teeth while eating Oreos.

Dachshund – an animal which is half a dog high by a dog and a half long.

Did you hear about the dyslexic agnostic insomniac who stays up all night wondering if there really is a Dog?

Dogs and cats instinctively know the exact moment their owners will wake up. Then they wake them 10 minutes sooner.

Dogs are better than children. Children are for people who can't have dogs.

Dogs are better than humans because they know but do not tell.

Dogs are lousy poker players. When they get a good hand they wag their tails.

Dogs are really people with fur coats.

Dogs believe they are human. Cats believe they are God.

Dog hair is just another condiment in my kitchen.

Dogs have owners, cats have staff.

Dogs lick you because they love you – cats lick you because you had chicken for dinner.

Dogs may shed, buts cats shred.

Dogs motivate us to play, be affectionate, seek adventure and be loyal.

Every boy who has a dog should also have a mother, so the dog can be fed regularly.

Every day is Saturday to a dog.

Every dog isn't a growler, and every growler isn't a dog.

Family and friends welcome. Fleas are not.

Four things a woman should know: How to look like a girl, how to act like a lady, how to think like a man, and how to work like a dog.

Great Dane: the kind of puppy that has the house broken before he is.

Great Dane

He is your friend, your partner, your defender, your dog. You are his life, his love, his leader. He will be yours, faithful and true to the last beat of his heart. You owe it to him to be worthy of such devotion.

I hope to be the kind of person my dog thinks I am.

I like dogs better (than people). They give you unconditional love. They either lick your face or bite you, but you will always know where they're coming from. With people, you never know which ones will bite.

If there are no dogs in Heaven, then when I die I want to go where they went.

If you can look at a dog and not feel vicarious excitement and affection, you must be a cat.

If you can resist treating a rich friend better than a poor friend,
If you can face the world without lies and deceit,
If you can say honestly that deep in your heart you have no prejudice against creed, color, religion or politics,
Then, my friend, you are almost as good as your dog.

If you want the best seat in the house ... move the dog.

If your dog doesn't like someone you probably shouldn't either.

If your dog is too fat, you are not getting enough exercise.

In a dog's world, silence means survival.

In a perfect world, every dog would have a home and every home would have a dog.

In dog years I'm dead.

In order to keep a true perspective of one's importance, everyone should have a dog that will worship him and a cat that will ignore him.

In order to successfully train a dog you must first be smarter than the dog.

It's no coincidence that man's best friend cannot talk.

Just because you have to work in a cube all day doesn't mean your dog has to sit in a crate all day.

Life is just one table scrap after another.

Lost: Dalmatian. Should be easy to spot.

Dalmatian

Maybe you've been looking for love in all the wrong places. A dog will treat you better than anyone you'll meet at happy hour.

My dog's not spoiled...I'm just well trained!

My sunshine doesn't come from the skies; it comes from the love in my dogs eyes.

Never judge a dog's pedigree by the kind of books he does not chew.

Never send a dog to deliver a steak.

Never trust a dog to watch your food.

DOG QUOTES

No matter what life brings you, take a lesson from your dog...kick some grass over that shit and move on.

One reason a dog can be such a comfort when you're feeling blue is that he doesn't try to find out why.

Recycle bones here.

So many people get reformed through religion. I'm reformed through my German shepherd.

Some days you're the dog, some days you're the hydrant.

Sorry, but my dog thinks you're an asshole, and I believe him.

Spouse and dog missing...25 cents reward for dog.

Support your local bloodhound. Get lost.

Bloodhound

Tail wagging the dog.

The dog at the entrance gate invariably reflects the personality of the people you will meet at the door.

The ideal dog food would be a ration that tastes like a postman.

The more people I meet the more I like my dog.

The reason a dog has so many friends is that he wags his tail instead of his tongue.

There is a direct correlation between a dog's behavior, and the state of its owner's mind.

There is no snooze button on a dog who wants breakfast.

There is only one smartest dog in the world, and every boy has it.

There's not much you can do with a terrier, ma'am.

To err is human, to forgive, canine.

Try throwing a ball just once for a dog. It would be like eating only one peanut or potato chip. Try to ignore the importuning of a Golden Retriever who has brought you his tennis ball, the greatest treasure he possesses.

Golden Retriever

When a dog wags its tail and barks at the same time, how do you know which end to believe?

When it's raining cats and dogs, be sure not to step in the poodles.

DOG QUOTES

When please doesn't work…Beg!

When you feel dog tired at night, it may be because you've growled all day long.

Work can wait another 30 minutes. There are more important things to do. Like throwing sticks.

You can't keep a good man down – or an over affectionate dog.

You do not own a dog, the dog owns you.

You never realize a dog is a man's best friend until you start betting on horses.

Chapter 10: Proverbs

A dog knows the places he is thrown food.
~ African Proverb

A stranger in town is like a white dog, he gets noticed immediately.
~ African Proverb

Do not call to a dog with a whip in your hand.
~ African Proverb

The lion does not turn around when a small dog barks.
~ African Proverb

A wise man associating with the vicious becomes an idiot; a dog traveling with good men becomes a rational being.
~ Arabian Proverb

The dogs may bark, but the caravan moves on.
~ Arabic Proverb

If a sane dog fights a mad dog, it's the sane dog's ear that is bitten off.
~ Burmese Proverb

A good dog does not block the road.
~ Chinese Proverb

Better to be a dog in times of peace than a human being in times of trouble.
~ Chinese Proverb

From the lowly perspective of a dog's eyes, everyone looks short.
~ Chinese Proverb

DOG QUOTES

One dog barks at something, the rest bark at him.
~ Chinese Proverb

Out of a dog's mouth will never come ivory tusks.
~ Chinese Proverb

The black dog gets the food; the white dog gets the blame.
~ Chinese Proverb

To be followed home by a stray dog is a sign of impending wealth.
~ Chinese Proverb

An honest man is not the worse because a dog barks at him.
~ Danish Proverb

Relatives are the worst friends, said the fox as the dogs took after him.
~ Danish Proverb

The dog's kennel is not the place to keep a sausage.
~ Danish Proverb

The barking of a dog does not disturb the man on a camel.
~ Egyptian Proverb

He that would hang his dog gives out first that he is mad.
~ English Proverb

It is home to a dog after he has been there three nights.
~ Finnish Proverb

A dog in the kitchen asks for no company.
~ French Proverb

The best thing about a man is his dog.
~ French Proverb

A fence lasts three years, a dog lasts three fences, a horse lasts three dogs, and a man lasts three horses.
~ German Proverb

The fatter the flea the leaner the dog.
~ German Proverb

The silent dog is the first to bite.
~ German Proverb

To live long, eat like a cat, drink like a dog.
~ German Proverb

Children aren't dogs; adults aren't gods.
~ Haitian Proverb

Only mad dogs and Englishman go out in the noonday sun.
~ Indian Proverb

A dog owns nothing, yet is seldom dissatisfied.
~ Irish Proverb

A dog with two homes is never any good.
~ Irish Proverb

It is bad to awaken a sleeping dog.
~ Italian Proverb

Those who sleep with dogs will rise with fleas.
~ Italian Proverb

If a man be great even his dog will wear a proud look.
~ Japanese Proverb

One dog yelping at nothing will set ten thousand straining at their collars.
~ Japanese Proverb

DOG QUOTES

A dog that steals sells its body.
~ Kenyan Proverb

Beware of a silent dog and still water.
~ Latin Proverb

The dog that fetches will also carry.
~ Latin Proverb

When the old dog barks it is time to watch.
~ Latin Proverb

While a dog gnaws the bone, companions would be none.
~ Latin Proverb

Do not respond to a barking dog.
~ Moroccan Jewish Proverb

Every animal knows more than you do.
~ Native American Proverb

The greater love is a mother's; then comes a dog's; then a sweetheart's.
~ Polish Proverb

A house without either a cat or a dog is the house of a scoundrel.
~ Portuguese Proverb

The dog wags his tail, not for you, but for your bread.
~ Portuguese Proverb

A dog has four feet, but he can't walk four different paths.
~ Proverb

A dog in a kennel barks at his fleas; a dog hunting does not notice them.
~ Proverb

A kitchen-dog is never a good rabbit-hunter.
~ Proverb

Dog does not eat dog.
~ Proverb

Give a dog a bad name and hang him.
~ Proverb

He who pelts every barking dog must pick up many stones.
~ Proverb

Hold your dog in readiness before you start the hare.
~ Proverb

If it were a dog, it would have bitten you already
~ Proverb

Many dogs kill a hare, no matter how many turns it makes.
~ Proverb

One barking dog sets the street barking.
~ Proverb

The hindmost dog may catch the hare.
~ Proverb

Why keep a dog and bark yourself?
~ Proverb

If you are a host to your guest, be a host to his dog also.
~ Russian Proverb

If you stop every time a dog barks, your road will never end.
~ Saudi Arabian Proverb

A collie has the brain of a man, and ways of a woman.
~ Scottish Proverb

DOG QUOTES

A dog that intends to bite does not bear its teeth.
~ Turkish Proverb

If skill could be gained by watching, every dog would become a butcher.
~ Turkish Proverb

A good dog deserves a good bone.
~ US Proverb

Even a dog knows the difference between being stumbled over and being kicked.
~ US Proverb

Every dog is allowed one bite.
~ US Proverb

If you play with the dog, he will lick your face.
~ Vietnamese Proverb

Three things it is best to avoid: a strange dog, a flood, and a man who thinks he is wise.
~ Welsh Proverb

A dog without teeth will also attack a bone.
~ Yiddish Proverb

Show a dog a finger and he wants the whole hand.
~ Yiddish Proverb

Chapter 11: Cross Breeding

Breed a Boxer with a German Shorthaired Pointer, you get a Boxershorts. A dog never seen in public.

Breed a Bulldog with a Shih Tzu and you get a Bullshitz.

Breed a Labrador Retriever with a Curly Coated Retriever, you get a Lab Coat Retriever. The choice for research scientists.

Mix a Newfoundland with a Bassett Hound, you get the Newfound Asset Hound. A dog for financial advisors.

Breed a Pointer with an Irish Setter, you get a Pointsetter. A traditional Christmas Pet.

Chapter 12: Dog Superstitions

Dogs have always been credited with the power of sensing supernatural influences, and seeing ghosts, spirits, fairies or deities which are invisible to human eyes. In Wales only dogs could see the death-brining hounds of Annwn; in ancient Greece the dogs were aware when Hecate was at a crossroads foretelling a death. Dogs are believed to be aware of the presence of ghosts, and their barking, whimpering or howling is often the first warning of supernatural occurrences.

There are many instances of black dog ghosts which are said to haunt lanes, bridges, crossroads, footpaths and gates, particularly in Suffolk, Norfolk and the Isle of Man. Some black dogs are said to be unquiet ghosts of wicked souls, but others are friendly guides and protectors to travelers; the Barguest of northern England could also appear as a pig or a goat, but was most commonly a hug black dog with large eyes and feet which left no prints. Packs of ghostly hounds have also been recorded all over Britain, often heard howling as they pass by on stormy nights rather than actually seen; these hounds generally foretell death, or at least disaster, if they are seen and the proper action is to drop face-down onto the ground to avoid spotting them.

When a dog howls in an otherwise silent night, it is said to be an omen of death, or at least of misfortune. A howling dog outside the house of a sick person was once thought to be an omen that they would die, especially if the dog was driven away and returned to howl again. A Dog which gives a single howl, or three howls, and then falls silent is said to be marking a death that has just occurred nearby.

Dogs were feared as possible carriers of rabies; sometimes even a healthy dog was killed if it had bitten someone, because of the belief that if the dog later developed rabies, even many years afterwards, the bitten person would also be afflicted. Remedies for the bite of a mad dog often included the patient being forced to eat a part of the dog in question, such as its hairs or a piece of its cooked liver. Dogs were also used to cure other illnesses; one old charm which was often used for children' illnesses was to take some of the patient's hairs and feed them to a dog in between slices of bread and butter; the ailment was believed to transfer to the animal, healing the patient.

In Scotland, a strange dog coming to the house means a new friendship; in England, to meet a spotted or black and white dog on your way to a business appointment is lucky. Three white dogs seen together are considered lucky in some areas; black dogs are generally considered unlucky, especially if they cross a traveler's path or follow someone and refuse to be driven away. Fisherman traditionally regard dogs as unlucky and will not take one out in a boat, or mention the word "dog" whilst at sea.

Chapter 13: Dog Tales

Dogs would make totally incompetent criminals. If you could somehow get a group of dogs to understand the concept of the Kennedy assassination, they would all immediately confess to it. Whereas you'll never see a cat display any kind of guilty behavior, despite the fact that several cats were seen in Dallas on the grassy knoll area, not that I wish to start any rumors.
~ Dave Barry

Lassie looked brilliant, in part because the farm family she lived with was made up of idiots. Remember? One of them was always getting pinned under the tractor, and Lassie was always rushing back to the farmhouse to alert the other ones. She'd whimper and tug at their sleeves, and they'd always waste precious minutes saying things: "Do you think something's wrong? Do you think she wants us to follow her? What is it, girl?" as if this had never happened before, instead of every week.

Lassie

What with all the time those people spent pinned under the tractor, I don't see how they managed to grow any crops

whatsoever. They probably got by on federal crop supports, which Lassie filed the applications for.
~ Dave Barry

I called our hotel but the response was "I'm sorry, sir. We've been booked up for months." With sudden inspiration, I called back. This time I said, "Hello, this is Shana's human..." and this time the response was, "Oh yes, sir. Come on down. We always have a room for you." It really puts you in your place when your dog can get a hotel room, but you can't.
~ J. Emmett Black, Jr., on how all the staff at a certain Holiday Inn knew his dog by name, but not him. Crime was reduced whenever Shana stayed there; she's a 120 pound Great Dane.

Great Dane

People always joke that "dog" spells "god" backwards. They should consider that it might be the higher power coming down to see just how well they do, what kind of people they are. The animals are right here, right in front of us. And how we treat these companions is a test.
~ Linda Blair

I'm a big man and I like big dogs...the dogs kept growing until only one of us could get in the elevator. It caused enough hassles so they finally kicked me out of my apartment.
~ Wilt Chamberlain, about living with two Great Danes in New York City

It looks like a miniature hippopotamus with badly fitting pantyhose all over.
~ On the Chinese Shar-pei

Chinese Shar-pei

One evening at Chequires the film was Oliver Twist. Rufus, as usual, had the best seat in the house, on his master's lap. At the point when Bill Sikes was about to drown his dog to put the police off his track, Churchill covered Rufus's eyes with his hand. He said, "Don't look now, dear. I'll tell you about it afterwards."
~ Winston Churchill, The Little Brown Book of Antecdotes

Like all celebrities, they've got a routine when on the road: first class seat (always right side, second row, window), a stretch limo waiting, the finest suites and Evian water.
~ Todd Copilevitz, writing about Nipper and Chipper, the RCA Jack Russell terriers

Many of us have to spell words such as "out," "cookie," and "bath" when conversing with other people, lest we unnecessarily excite our pets. And even then they often understand. I've actually had clients who resorted to using a second language around their dogs, but after a while their perceptive pooches caught on. Who says dogs don't understand us?
~ Warren Eckstein

The friendship of a dog is precious. It becomes even more so when one is so far removed from home. I have a Scottie. In him I find consolation and diversion...he is the "one person" to whom I can talk without the conversation coming back to war.
~ Dwight D. Eisenhower

Thomas A. Edison was once reluctantly persuaded by his wife to attend one of the big social functions of the season in New York. At last the inventor managed to escape the crowd of people vying for his attention, and sat alone unnoticed in a corner. Edison kept looking at his watch with a resigned expression on his face. A friend edged near to him unnoticed and heard the inventor mutter to himself with a sigh, "If there were only a dog here!"
~ Edmund Fuller

A study conducted by the State University of New York at Buffalo Medical School suggested that in times of stress a dog is likely to be more help in calming you down than a spouse or partner. Most dog owners can guess the reason why: dogs never judge us and never compete with us.
~ Marjorie Garber

I read the Odyssey because it was the story of a man who returned home after being absent for more than twenty years and was recognized only by this dog.
~ Guillermo C. Infante

Golden retrievers are not bred to be guard dogs, and considering the size of their hearts and their irrepressible joy in life, they are less likely to bite than to bark, less likely to bark than to lick a hand in greeting. In spite of their size, they think they are lap dogs, and in spite of being dogs, they think they are also human, and nearly every human they meet is judged to have the potential to be a soon companion who might, at any moment, cry, "Let's go!" and lead them on a great adventure.
~ Dean Koontz

A Canadian psychologist is selling a video that teaches you how to test your dog's IQ. Here's how it works: if you spend $12.99 for the video, your dog is smarter than you.
~ Jay Leno

When I got him out he was near froze solid and shivering. He was shaking so hard that I wasted half a glass of whiskey trying to aim it for his mouth. Must have got enough of it into him, though, since it did seem to bring him back to life.
~ Abraham Lincoln, on what it took to save his dog after pulling him from a river where he went through thin ice.

When a human dies, there is a Bridge they must cross to enter into heaven. At the head of that bridge waits every animal that human encountered during their lifetime. The animals, based upon what they know of this person, decide which humans may cross the bridge and which will be turned away.
~ Native American Legend

My name is Oprah Winfrey. I have a talk show. I'm single. I have eight dogs – five golden retrievers, two black labs, and a mongrel. I have four years of college.
~ Oprah Winfrey, when asked to describe herself during jury selection.

DOG QUOTES

Old Yeller was bought for 3 dollars from a shelter; his real name was Spike.
~ World Features

Disney's "Shaggy Dog" was bought for 2 dollars at a pound.
~ World Features

A guy wanted the vet to cut his dog's tail off. The vet asked why.
"Well, my mother-in-law is visiting next month and I want to eliminate any possible indication that she is welcome."

I've been in the hotel business over thirty years. Never yet have I called the police to eject a disorderly dog during the small hours of the night. Never yet has a dog set the bedclothes afire from smoking a cigarette. I've never found a hotel towel or blanket in a dog's suitcase, nor whiskey rings on the bureau top from a dog's bottle. Sure the dog's welcome.
P.S. If he'll vouch for you, come along too.
~ Unknown hotel manager's reply to a vacationer writing to ask if dogs were permitted

MEET THE AUTHOR

Amy and Cozmo

Amy Morford has over twenty years of dog training experience with companion dogs, sport dogs and working breeds. Amy's motivation to write about dogs stems from her love for them and their unbiased loyalty and devotion. Amy's goal is to provide helpful, accurate information to assist dog lovers with raising and training a well-mannered, good-tempered, happy, healthy, well-adjusted companion, friend, partner and/or family pet.

Be sure to bookmark and subscribe to Check out DogTrainingPlace.net for dog training tips and over 10,000 name ideas. Happy Dog Training!

More Books by Amy Morford

Dog Eldercare: Caring For Your Middle Aged to Older Dog

DoggyPedia: All You Need To Know About Dogs

How to Speak Dog: Dog Training Simplified For Dog Owners

Pet Names and Numerology: Choose the Right Name For Your Pet

Puppy Training: From Day 1 to Adulthood (How to Make Your Puppy Loving and Obedient)

Scared Dog Audio

The German Shepherd Big Book: All About The German Shepherd Breed